My First B[ook About]
Go[ats]

Amazing An[imal]
Children's Picture Books

By Molly Davidson
Mendon Cottage Books

JD-Biz Publishing

Download Free Books!
http://MendonCottageBooks.com

Read More Amazing Animal Books

Purchase at Amazon.com

Download Free Books!
http://MendonCottageBooks.com

Table of Contents

Introduction

Goats are very picky eaters, even though most people think they eat everything.

Goats have been owned and used by humans for food and clothes for thousands of years.

Sheep, antelope, and goats are all cousins.

What are goats?

Goats have been owned by humans for as long as we know, probably as long as cats, dogs, and horses.

There are more goats in China than anywhere else in the World.

A goat and a kid in a meadow

Goats have a cloven foot, which means it is split down the middle.

An adult girl goat is called a nanny or a doe, a baby goat is called a kid, and an adult boy is called a buck or a billy goat.

There are over 300 different breeds of goats.

Most are about the size of a Labrador retriever dog.

Goats and humans

A boy feeding a goat

Goats are usually kept in herds, and in many countries, the children and teenagers watch over the goats.

In the summer goats are allowed to roam around in a pasture, so they can eat grass.

Many farmers will bring their goats into a barn, so some shelter in the winter, to help keep them warm.

A goat herdsman in the Serengeti

Goats are used mostly for their milk and meat.

Goats first came to America with Christopher Columbus, an explorer of America.

What do goats eat?

Many people think goats will eat anything, but they are picky eaters, they will try to eat anything, but that doesn't mean they eat it.

A goat eating grass

Goats like to eat grass, alfalfa, hay, and weeds.

Goats will not eat anything that is dirty, so if it has mud or dirt on it, they won't eat it.

Goats also need salt, which they lick from a salt block.

Just like most animals they also need water; the plants they eat don't give them enough.

Goats have four stomachs which help digest all the plants they eat

What Goats Look Like

Goats don't have fur, they have different kinds of hair, some shaggy, curly, and short.

Goats have horns, which they use for fighting each other.

Goats' eyes are horizontal (sideways) instead of most animals that are vertical (up and down).

A goat's eye

Many goats have floppy ears, but some have straight ears.

They have a split upper lip, this is used for grabbing things, this helps them explore.

Boy and girl goats can have a beard, and many also have a waddle (it is a piece of skin hanging from their chin).

They do not have teeth on their top front jaw, just on the bottom.

How do goats act?

Goats are very social; they like to live in herds with many other goats.

A baby goat (kid) stays in its mother for about 5 months before it is born.

A mother goat can have 1 - 6 kids at a time.

Kids drink their mother's milk for about 2 or 3 months, but it also starts eating grass when it is only 2 weeks old.

Kids are said to be an adult goat at 6 months old.

Goats fight by butting heads, this is to show who is boss or to impress a girl.

Goats are smart; they like to escape from their pens, by jumping over or ramming the gate until it breaks.

Goats do not like to get rained on. They always run for shelter, to help keep them dry.

Goats can jump up to 5 feet, and some even climb trees.

The sounds they make are called a bleat. They can be soft or loud, and some even sound like words, but they cannot speak like a human.

Goats have very good balance, much better than humans.

Pygmy Goats

Pygmy goats are one of the smallest goats, they weigh between 50 - 80 pounds.

They are very common in Africa.

A pygmy goat

Pygmy goats are a very popular pet, and used many times for petting zoos.

They can learn to live in almost any climate, and are very calm.

Australian Goats

Australian goats actually came from Britain, when Australia first became a country.

Many goats escaped or were set free; these goats then made wild herds.

Paul Esson © <u>Wikimedia Commons</u>

These wild goat herds have become a problem, since they don't really have any predators, because they were brought to Australia, they are not from there.

They keep having kids and making more goats, they are eating all the wild grass and shrubs.

Charles Esson © <u>Wikimedia Commons</u>

Australian goats can be helpful, the ones that are domesticated (owned by humans) are used for their hair, eaten for meat, milked, and are sold as a business.

Boer Goats

Boer goats are one of the biggest goats; they can weigh up to 300 pounds.

Boer goat

Boer goats were first from South Arica, the word "boer" is a farmer in South Africa.

Boer goats are mainly used as meat, they are not milked and their hair isn't used for clothes.

American LaMancha Goats

LaMancha goats are the only goat breed from America.

A woman named Mrs. Eula Fay Frey first bred them in the 1950's.

American LaMancha Goat

They have really short ears; which are called gopher or elf ears.

Dwarf Goats

Dwarf goats are the smallest goat; they weigh about 20 pounds.

Besides being smaller, they are just like regular goats, and are used for milk.

An African dwarf goat on a farm

They were first brought to America, as food for lions and tigers in the zoo.

Landrace Goats

Landrace is a word that means native to the area.

Landrace goats have been in the place they live basically forever.

A pair of Dutch landrace goats

All of these goats live in colder climates, and have longer hair.

Alpine Goats

Steven Walling © <u>Wikimedia Commons</u>

Alpine goats live in the French Alps; these are mountains in France, Italy, and Switzerland.

Alpine goats are used as food by many people that live in the mountains; sine there is not really any place to grow crops.

Elena Tartaglione © <u>Wikimedia Commons</u>

Alpine goats produce a lot of milk; which is used for cheese, ice cream, soap, and other things.

Their hair is known as pied, which means spotted.

Angora Goats

Angora goats have curly hair, it looks shaggy and messy.

An angora goat

Angora goats' hair is used for fabric, it is very soft, and is used to make things like sweaters and blankets.

They come from Turkey, and they were so important they were on the back on one of their coins.

Cashmere Goats

Cashmere goats are also known for their soft hair.

They mostly live in China and India.

A cashmere goat

Cashmere goats have two layers of hair, the outer layer that's for protection all year long, and the under layer which is grown just for winter, this layer is cashmere.

Charles Esson © <u>Wikimedia Commons</u>

Mountain Goats

Mountain goats aren't true goats; they have good balance and split toes like them.

They live high in the mountains of North America; this is where they were found by English explorers, who gave them their name.

A mountain goat and a kid

One difference between a mountain goat and a regular goat is mountain goats have never been owned by people, they are all wild.

They also have something special on their hooves; they are sharp bits that help them hold on to the rocks of the mountain.

They like to fight way more than regular goats, and sometimes they really hurt each other.

Conclusion

Goats milk is the most common milk drank by people all over the World.

Not very many people are allergic to goat's milk, even people who are allergic to cow's milk.

Goat is also eaten more than other meats, because goats are cheaper to take care of than bigger animals, like cows and pigs.

Download Free Books!
http://MendonCottageBooks.com

Purchase at Amazon.com
Website http://AmazingAnimalBooks.com

Our books are available at

1. Amazon.com

2. Barnes and Noble

3. Itunes

4. Kobo

5. Smashwords

6. Google Play Books

Download Free Books!
http://MendonCottageBooks.com

Publisher

JD-Biz Corp

P O Box 374

Mendon, Utah 84325

http://www.jd-biz.com/

Mendon Cottage Books
P O Box 374, Mendon Utah 84325

22284941R00025

Printed in Great Britain
by Amazon